ONDAS

2020 COLLECTION

ONDAS

2020 COLLECTION

Manifestations from beyond
eclipsing the darkness of ignorance,
revealing the light of awareness.

TITO PÉREZ

Library of Congress Number: 2021905049

Paperback: 978-1-7367870-0-7
E-book: 978-1-7367870-1-4
Audio: 978-1-7367870-4-5

Publisher
A-zWizzard Productions, LLC
P.O. Box 18134
Corpus Christi, TX 78480
AzWizzard.com

Cover and Interior Design: Creative Publishing Book Design
Author Photograph: Ryan Perez

Special thanks to my long-time friend David Vogler who helped me with editing and revising the original Ondas when they first started happening to me years ago and to my good friend and mentor Professor Stephan Sencerz for his invaluable and insightful guidance when I was trying to sort things out but kept bumping into things.

I asked,
"What am I supposed to do with these?"
I was told,
"Share them with the world."

Tito Pérez

ONDAS
2020 COLLECTION

INTRODUCTION

"Onda" is a Spanish word with several meanings, one of which is a colloquial expression signifying an insight, delivered in brief commentaries expressing myriad thoughts, observations and expressions.

I consider every Onda in this book an insight, each occurring spontaneously and extemporaneously. I could make the untrue claim that these messages result after careful and thoughtful contemplation and deliberation. But, they do not. Ondas just happen. They just come to me. As of this writing, they number in the thousands. (I explain how I came up with the "Ondas" name in the History section.)

As much as I will try to explain the origins, structure, and nature of these Ondas, the foundation for my thoughts are supported by intangible feelings and senses, as well as by elusive intuition. Further, I believe that I am no one special and that everyone has been experiencing Ondas all along, but most have either not heeded or completely dismissed these messages.

My simple mission is to spread these Ondas all over the world. During the process, I will make the argument that what has and is happening to me has been happening to others for eons and throughout the modern era. I will also argue that given the right conditions, you too can begin to recognize and embrace your own Ondas and perhaps one day also share with others all over the world.

HISTORY

Around August of 1998, I was sitting on my patio reading, writing and listening to music. Suddenly I began to experience inclusive, brief images that I thought were ideas for future poems. Grabbing my pen and pad, I began to write down these thoughts. A few weeks later, after scripting a few hundred pieces, I began to realize that there was something different about these "notes" that I was penning as though I was taking dictation. The brief, short messages spoke for themselves, not seeming to need further expansion or clarification. It was then that I began to seriously question the nature of just what it was I was writing.

I decided to visit with a long-time friend, an ex-newspaper editor, to get his opinion on these short pieces of prose that just kept popping into my head. My friend suggested that my writings where a mix of aphorisms, maxims and quips. I disagreed with all his suggestions. He did not seem to be able to grasp, or accept, the concept that these messages were coming through me and not from me. If they had been my original thoughts, then I would have easily accepted the notion that the literature could possibly be classified as aphorisms, maxims or quips. But, if these written pieces were not coming from me, my most pressing question was, "Where were these thoughts coming from?"

I remember returning home a little frustrated and headed straight to my patio to reflect on the matter some more. I remember the exact moment when I was looking down at a notebook full of the writings and, exasperated, asked myself, "What are these Ondas?" "That's it!" I said. "They are Ondas!" I immediately associated the term Ondas with insights. From that point on things began to become a little more, though not totally, clear.

ORIGINS

The ideas that follow are my thoughts on the origins of Ondas — thoughts influenced, shaped, and maybe even warped, by my senses and intuition. I know the Ondas are not emanating from within me (even the ego-less me); I know the messages, the thoughts, the ideas are as new to me as to those who may be reading them for the first time. Oddly, by detaching myself from the Ondas (accepting they did not originate from within or at least not from my conscious self) I seemed to connect with them even more.

In the History section, I shared thoughts on why I felt I am conveying and not originating Ondas. Simply, the Ondas come through me and I record them (sometimes in disjointed bits and pieces.) Further, I do not believe that I am anyone special or, even worse, someone "chosen" to record and catalogue Onda-type messages. I believe that everyone is a conduit for Ondas, but not everyone is listening or receptive to Ondas when and as they manifest themselves. We each have the ability to be channels for Ondas because we are all, in varying degrees, psychic (connected to an enigmatic, mystical, all-pervasive energy source) and, consequently, each possesses a natural, innate ability to convey Ondas.

So, if these Ondas were not originating from the self, or its higher consciousness as some might argue, then where were they coming from? Who or what was doing the conveying? Though I have given these questions much thought, reflecting on several possible answers, everything that follows is, nonetheless, speculative—my ideas influenced by an intertwining conglomeration of intuitions, instincts and senses. If my views are construed by some as lunacy, delusional, absurd or nonsensical, I may not be in a position to argue otherwise. In spite of these and other risks, the following are my thoughts on the origins of Ondas.

I believe the Ondas are originating from a divine energy that some consider a supreme consciousness (universal mind) whose character and composition are unfathomable, unimaginable and inconceivable. I, therefore, do not try to discern the nature, intent or desire of that which is beyond my ability to comprehend or conceptualize. Some may argue that the supreme consciousness is a god; but, entering that realm exposes you to the possibility of accepting others' understandings of that god's nature, disposition and wants. Ondas neither express demands nor propose truths or argue issues. So, how then can a god be in the equation?

Accepting that an intractable connection exists between the ideas of an omniscient god and a universal supreme consciousness compels one to rethink accepted notions of what a god really is. It is much easier to acquiesce to and consider plausible the proposition that Ondas are coming from a god defined as the ultimate enigma, and not necessarily the god(s) defined by various religions. However, making this association would put Ondas in harm's way of becoming dogmatic and, consequently, it is more prudent to accept that the answer to the question of where Ondas come from is only a guess. Not knowing the point of origin makes it difficult to ascertain why Ondas manifest and for what purpose. What follows are my thoughts and possible answers.

NATURE

The intrinsic nature of the Ondas indicate that some energy (a supreme consciousness, a Great Spirit, a god, the divine, or any other characterization of that pervasive energy that connects all of creation) is allowing for the manifestation of thoughts, observations and ideas to increase universal awareness. There are no directives, missives or dictates; and, therefore, there are no demands made on the reader to accept the messages in the Ondas. I surmise that an unknowable pervasive energy (everyone is free to call it what they want) is the source that is presenting an opportunity to expand humanity's perceptions, but only so far as it is willing, or even able, to venture beyond its own individual perceptual boundaries.

Though some Ondas espouse that ultimately everyone is accountable for their actions, the consequences for not accepting or believing the content of the messages are nil. Understanding the origins or the genesis of Ondas may not be as important as accepting that they exist and are coming into one's mind from an external source. Note that "external source" does not necessarily mean that that source is not also an integral part of your very being. Because of their nature, my hypothesis is that Ondas are originating from an enigmatic divine energy, and that whatever the intention, it is motivated by goodness, if not by love.

CHARACTER

Besides their intrinsic attributes, all Ondas have common, distinct elements. They express realities in ways that may not have been considered before or are contrary to established beliefs. This is not to say that revealing an unseen or long forgotten facet of a particular reality will make a newer reality any more acceptable. If you are raised to believe an age-old notion that sacrificing a goat on the winter solstice will ensure a plentiful spring crop, then any evidence or facts to the contrary will do little to change those engrained and entrenched memes (perceptions, conceptions and notions commonly accepted as reality by societal mores or culture). In these instances, lamentably, goats will continue to die needlessly.

Further, if someone is brought up to believe that the earth was created several thousand years ago, then no scientific evidence, regardless of how compelling and overwhelming, will change entrenched perceptions and beliefs. In these, and similar instances, it is lamentable that ignorance continues to extend its roots into the psyche; reigning supreme over reason and fact. Such is the power of faith, anchored by dogma over facts; of engrained beliefs, intertwined with ancient notions over reason; of unquestioned, inviolate perceptions that attempt to suppress one's innate desires to explore and discover, over truth.

Among other things, I believe Ondas increase one's awareness by encouraging the juxtaposition of reality with reason. Joined, that chemistry can create sparks that ignite flames of understanding; illuminating and making evident that which was unknown. In the light of this awareness, things not supported by empirical evidence are respectfully, but steadfastly, challenged, examined and otherwise submitted to rigorous critical review and analysis. One Onda reads,

WRIT

Because it has

Been written,

Does not make

It so;

Because it

Is so,

Does not mean

It has

Been written.

(This applies to Ondas, too.) A corollary to this Onda might remind us that because someone says it is so, does not make it so.

The brevity of Ondas might compel some to think that the source (originator) is somewhat of a word miser, using words sparingly as if in short supply. Ondas make one point and deliver one message at a time. Ondas may convey different aspects of a particular theme (e.g., varying views on love) but the messages are still unique. There have been times when I have had to double-check to ensure no repetition of earlier messages. Can you repeat or restate Ondas? It is possible, but I firmly believe the same or similar Onda can come to others at the same time or on different levels.

It would be useless to attempt to write a treatise on the character of Ondas; because, in the end, it would all still be conjecture. Ondas are insights and since it is not possible to define the nature of a particular insight until it occurs, so, too, it is with an Onda. Whatever makes an insight an insight makes an Onda an Onda — each appears meant to increase awareness; and, all come unexpectedly and effortlessly. The true genesis of Ondas may remain unknown. Perhaps one day the innate character of Ondas will be explored and definitive attributes validated and identified. When or whether that will happen is anyone's guess, but if it does happen, I believe that it will be long after my passing.

EXPOSITION

As mentioned before, the term Ondas is colloquial Spanish for insights. The ethereal nature of an Onda enables it to be viewed as a noun (insight) or an adjective (insightful).

The organic definition of an Onda is that it is a thought, idea or expression manifesting in the conscious mind not as a result of any internal motivations, prejudices, biases, etc., or external events, influences, experiences, etc., or other stimuli. Ondas emanate from outside the self, and, I believe, are meant to help the conscious mind increase awareness and subsequent understanding; to stimulate critical, objective and analytical thinking; and, to bring a sense of comfort and peace, knowing that you are connected and connecting with an entity greater than yourself. (Perhaps this is the reason there are Ondas that manifest in the form of prayers.)

Trying to describe Ondas is further complicated by the very structure of Ondas as a group — I have identified ten distinct categories: **Emotions, Humanity, Inspirational, Karma, Nature, Prayers, Questions, Spiritual, The Self, and Zen-Mysticism.** As important as it was to try to define Ondas in general terms, it was just as important to describe and define each of the ten Onda categories, as well. Although I attempted to make the descriptions and definitions as concise and clear as possible, I am still struggling to grasp the Ondas' full meaning and purpose. I look forward to hearing from others who may have different views and observations.

The front page of this book reads "*Ondas: Manifestations from beyond; eclipsing the darkness of ignorance, revealing the light of awareness.*" These thoughts express the core nature and purpose of Ondas—where they come from and where they are going. What these thoughts do not do is detail specific attributes that make Ondas easier to identify. Understanding what an Ondas is becomes crucial if anyone is to be convinced that they, too, can experience Ondas.

The ability for you to recognize and record Ondas in your life will only happen if you know how to differentiate between your thoughts emanating from within and influenced by respective beliefs, perceptions and attitudes, and "manifestations from beyond"—thoughts and ideas that originate from outside the self. The difficulty is that like multi-faceted crystals, Ondas have many reflections; many ways they can be viewed, observed and experienced.

So, the most pressing question is, "How does one know an Onda when they see or hear one or when one happens (manifests) to them?" I am not sure that the general assessment on Ondas that follows will resolve or answer this, and possibly other questions; nor am I convinced that the true nature of Ondas will ever be known. What follows is a step toward attempting to discover some semblance of the empirical reality of Ondas.

The composition of Ondas, at least those that I experience, comes in the form of waves or pulses. Generally, though not all the time, they do not come in one complete stream of thought. Coincidently, the term Ondas is also Spanish for waves (as in ocean). The reception of Ondas in waves or pulses explains their written structure that, much like poems, has line breaks. So, instead of writing an Onda in one continuous line such as in *"LISTEN—Communications is a bridge one should be able to cross from either side."* the Onda is written:

LISTEN
Communication
Is a bridge
One should
Be able to cross
From either side.

Or,

"ERROR — I err, thereof, I am human." reads:

ERROR
I err,
Therefore,
I am human.

Because I am experiencing Ondas in waves or pulses does not necessarily mean everyone else will, too. Yet, as I read the Ondas with their particular structures, I cannot but help feel that I am being "fed" the Ondas in small portions and not in big gulps. It is these small "bites" that I record a line at a time, coming together to form a complete message, each with its own particular line structure. The final form of most Ondas has centered lines. The centering is intuitive and appears to improve readability and understanding.

Ondas sometimes come in pieces and do not necessarily form in a logical order. You sense the spirit of the Onda and then you have to take the pieces and rearrange and sometimes edit, or rewrite, the Onda to conform to the thought being expressed and sensed. An Onda might come in the following form:

Future not to predict,
Future to create.

to then be written:

BEGET
The future is
Not to predict,
But to create.

In effect, one might have to bevel and polish, like a fine jewel, an Onda until its clarity (the message) becomes clear. Forming or bringing together an Onda sometimes requires effort, patience and persistence. Often, the "jewel" comes into the mind ready to be "showcased" in its final form, without modification. Onda prayers, in particular, usually come (at least to me) "ready to go" with little, if any, tweaking necessary.

Where do the titles for the Ondas come from? I did not decide to start adding titles to Ondas until about 15 years after I had already written thousands of them. I felt that titles would add to the uniqueness of each Onda. To come up with a title, I reflect on the message and then on an appropriate, related title. And, the title cannot be a word pulled from the Onda itself (e.g., if the term "love" is already in the body of the Onda, it cannot be used for the title) so I have to find related words like "loving," "loved," "lovers," etc., or find another term altogether. I consider whether the title I chose is appropriate and whether I really want to use it on a particular Onda. The biggest strategic hurdle is coming up with a unique title for each Onda. Because I have thousands, to be able to come up with different titles for each is in itself a formidable challenge. I may even have to reach out to you, the reader, for ideas.

What follows are some of the attributes and characteristics I have identified in Ondas.

Ondas are:

1. **Spontaneous:** Thoughts are manifested independently; not precipitated or created by any conscious or deliberate thought processes or that have arisen because of an event. Ondas just happen or else they are not Ondas but, instead, induced or self-generated thoughts and ideas that, although insightful, are not extemporaneous.

2. **Enigmatic:** Though some take the form of prayers or are spiritual in nature, Ondas are nonetheless secular

in that they do not endorse, reinforce or reflect religious dogmas, creeds or convictions. Although they appear to be emanating from a higher, transcendent consciousness, Ondas do not express godly dictates, nor do they make claims of any godly desires. Further, they make no effort to define or to assign attributes and character to a god.

3. **Universal:** The messages emanating from each Onda address humanity in general, without preference to any particular group. Messages that are myopic and restrictive (i.e., favoring one belief system or religion, etc.,) that exhibit clear signs of influences of the "Us" versus "Them" attitudes common to judgmental, prejudiced and biased mentalities are easy to identify—Transparent intolerance, contempt and animosity represent the antithesis of Ondas.

4. **Deferential:** Even though some Ondas are iconoclastic in that they challenge, contradict and question established norms, conventions and belief systems, they do not condemn, ridicule or criticize in the process. Messages laced with tirades or that use labels to convey displeasure and disapproval can only emanate from the self and are not, by definition or character, Ondas.

Ondas are not:

1. **Prejudiced:** Ondas are neither influenced by or reflective of respective societal customs and conventions;

neither do they imitate or reiterate local beliefs, attitudes or perceptions. Messages of these sorts are often banal and sometimes represent internalized thoughts and expressions of ideas and notions that mirror unquestioned traditions, unsubstantiated beliefs or entrenched biases and prejudices.

2. **Judgmental:** Ondas are not about judgments, criticisms or condemnations. To offer judgment is to assume a posture of authoritative knowledge or superior comprehension and then use that perceived foundation as a basis for seeking to correct or make right some perceived error or wrong and/or to punish offenders. Ondas make no claim to know what is good or bad or offer answers on what is right or wrong. If Ondas succeed in awakening your own sense of connectivity to all humanity, the proposition is that you will recognize those answers on your own.

3. **Commandments:** There are no "Thou shall" or "Thou shall not" Ondas. There are only observations, introspections and reflections; letting the reader determine whether to accept or reject the messages, without fear of adverse consequences or without expectations of rewards. Without commanding, there are Ondas on Karma that intimate that in one way or another each one of us is accountable for our choices and actions. However, even in these cases there is no attempt to

judge. Ondas on Karma reflect on the notion that, as in physics, for every action there is a separate but equal reaction; and, further, that the consequent reaction can occur even after one's death. Simply, these Ondas on Karma seem to say that it is inevitable that those that do good will feel the good and those that do harm will feel the harm. In an indirect way, these Ondas indicate that in knowing we are each accountable, we should be diligent in commanding ourselves and be cautious when letting others command us.

ONDA CATEGORIES

EMOTIONS: What makes us most human is our ability to feel varying degrees of sometimes complex, confusing and overwhelming sensations. Emotions are the offspring of perceptions influenced by culture, society and tradition — triple Gordian knots. Where we call home and whom we live with, as well as the conditions we live in, influence and often determine whether a particular emotion will drive us to madness and destructive behavior, or whether the emotion will cause us to be more positive and constructive — becoming an energy that can uplift and invigorate. Emotions can debilitate and can empower. Who and what we are determines whether our emotions serve or destroy us, and maybe those around us, or whether they become catalysts that foster contentment and joy for others and ourselves.

Ondas relating to emotions are ruminative and contemplative, reflecting the myriad of helpful and harmful feelings exhibited by humans. As with all Ondas, these messages are not accusatory, condemning or judgmental.

HUMANITY: What is it that compels one human to ask of another, "Where is your humanity?" Posed in a different way, perhaps the question would more clearly elicit the knowledge sought, "What is your humanity?" The scientific notions of what makes one human are well documented: cultural and societal memes influence the myriad ways that humans answer these questions for themselves and might provide the definitive information necessary to assess just how "human" one is. However, even these questions may not be sufficient to determine one's true humanity.

Ondas addressing humanity focus on the oneness, likeness and similarities of humanity; revealing commonalities that make humans more kindred than some would admit; and, especially, less dissimilar, than some have been led to believe. These Ondas transcend the diverse views of cultures and societies influenced by respective customs, traditions and conventions that are not predicated on reason or science. Though lacking scientific discipline, the arguments and reasoning behind these Ondas still compel reflection and consideration.

INSPIRATIONAL: Inspire: to encourage or stimulate; an event or thought that enables one to ascend to a higher physical, mental or spiritual level. As much as you may try, it is difficult, if not impossible, to determine what, and how much, inspires or does not inspire. Someone in the throes of depression might need a lot more inspiration to climb out of their valley than someone who already feels good and is nearing their summit. States of mind, attitudes and beliefs influence and determine just how receptive one is to any form of inspiration. Moreover, simply defining inspiration does little to help one find inspiration.

Inspirational Ondas attempt to inspire by elevating one's awareness and cognizance to an extent one begins to believe in themselves and their ability to find their answers, their sense of purpose, and to clarify what they seek in their life. In the end, what inspires us may be nothing more than discovering that which gives us reason for wanting to exist, strive and succeed.

KARMA: Some hold that the positive and the negative aspects of Karma are addressed through successive lifetimes until a balance or reconciliation is achieved. Others lean in the direction that Karma is immediate, occurring in this lifetime and continuing after death. In either case, the proposition is that Karma is inevitable. Ondas seem to indicate that Karma proposes neither a terrible Hell (although one's Karmic experiences could provide a reasonable approximation) nor a hedonist's Heaven (unless feelings of joy and contentment can be considered hedonistic pleasures). Talk of Heaven and Hell as destinations and definite realities have pre-dated written text. Generally, the proposition is simply that you will wind up in one place or the other dependent on whether you were good or bad. But, the problem with these standards of reward or punishment is the reliance on following someone or something else's conception of what determines appropriate or inappropriate behavior, as well as what constitutes Heaven and Hell. Karma is more fundamental and simpler—you feel the totality of the bad or the good that you have caused. There is no judgment, no reward and no retribution—just consequence. You literally feel every instance of sorrow or happiness you have caused. With Karma, you create your own Heaven or Hell; you harvest the sweet or bitter fruit that you have sown. As such, Heavens and Hells are unique, their composition (lands of milk and honey or fiery, eternal pits of Hell) determined by the collective consequences of your individual acts on the temporal plane.

Ondas on Karma reflect on a dispassionate and non-judgmental force that is as dynamic and natural a process as any that exists in the universe. The best corollary to describe the Karmic process is to relate it to one of Newton's Laws of Motion—for every action there is a separate, but equal, reaction. With Karma, if the subsequent reaction does not occur while one is alive, it will after death. Karma is unavoidable.

NATURE: Nature is the totality of existence. It is the macrocosm (planets, galaxies, black holes, dark matter, etc.) and microcosm (humans, societies, biomass, ecological interrelatedness, etc.) as well as the physical laws that explain and provide empirical definitions of reality (gravity, electromagnetism, strong/weak nuclear forces.) Understanding nature is important for survival while ignorance of nature exposes us to potentially dire consequences.

Ondas on Nature involve observations and conclusions relating to humanity's effects on nature and the expectant results and consequences. Though nature is everything around us, including the air we breathe, it is often taken for granted; dismissed as something that will always be. History and present-day experiences indicate an alternate reality.

PRAYERS: Whether or not there is a deity that answers or listens to one's supplications, invocations or affirmations may not be as important as the affect prayers have on the psyche and on one's spiritual state of awareness. When one uses prayer, they reach out and acknowledge they are a part of something greater than the self. It is to that higher power to which they turn for succor, direction and guidance. Differences and disputes defining and explaining the essence of that higher power have led to untold human misery and ruination.

Prayer Ondas are easy to recognize — each is directed toward anyone's God or Great Spirit without an attempt to define the nature of those undefinable and inexplicable entities seen as "greater than ourselves." Prayers are conveyed to an entity that even in its simplest form is an illimitable force beyond comprehension that can be sensed but never known, that can be touched but never affected or effected. In refusing to accept the notion that the something "greater than ourselves" is inconceivable and unfathomable, humanity consigns itself to continued disharmony trying to prove otherwise.

QUESTIONS: As soon as they recognized and accepted the notion of "self," ancient ancestors started to ask questions about themselves, including a still continuing effort to try to understand the reason for existence and the nature of their very being. Thus, they began to discover themselves and the world around them. Embedded in each question was a potential seed of discovery. Questions probed, inquired or compelled. In each case, the aim was discovery. Discovery became the watershed of knowledge. Without the continued expansion of knowledge, the mind and spirit will eventually stagnate and deteriorate. Questioning ensures intellectual and spiritual survival.

Onda questions can be contemplative, reflective or introspective. Sometimes a question does not solicit an immediate answer and serves more as a catalyst to precipitate more questions and more subsequent answers. As our knowledge increases, so does our drive to learn more. Like the ocean tides, the ebbing and flowing of questions and answers creates a dynamic process that ensures vibrancy and vitality. Those who would prohibit questions also seek to restrict the tide of discovery, an unnatural and unhealthy condition that can portend the formation of brackish, pestilent backwaters of ignorance.

SPIRITUAL: Unlike our tangible, corporeal nature, our spiritual self is not as easy to identify, quantify or measure. The moment we became cognizant of our physical selves, we also began to recognize that there was something more to us than mere flesh and blood. What that something is remains open to debate and question, but few can deny the feeling of spirit. We sense that there is an esoteric aspect about us that we cannot readily identify; nonetheless, we believe it is an integral part of our being.

Ondas on spirituality acknowledge the metaphysical—the existence of an innate transcendental nature that makes each unique, yet, the same with everything else within the vastness of creation. Understanding our connectivity with all of nature, with everything that exists, creates the awareness that helps us understand our spirituality. Once we are in touch with our spirit self, understanding our humanity and kinship with others becomes much easier. Our spirituality links us to all of existence; it forms the bridge from somewhere else to our humanity; it is what makes us more than one.

THE SELF: Rene Descartes wrote, "Cogito, ergo sum." (I think, therefore, I am.) Perhaps this was the first time someone had attempted to validate their existence by recognizing, empirically, the sentience in their nature. The quest for self-discovery has continued unabated ever since. Psychoanalysis is only one tool that continues the search to comprehend our complex, enigmatic and, often, fragile selves. We are continually evolving and changing; therefore, it seems that we may only know our true nature by reference to minute, fleeting moments in time.

Ondas on the Self relate to and acknowledge the complexities associated with understanding our mosaic selves while reflecting on how, as humans, we are so much alike. Becoming self-aware reduces our apathy and increases our empathy. Discovering ourselves helps us become aware of our true nature, connectivity and interrelatedness with other sentient beings.

ZEN-MYSTICISM: Zen: Reaching enlightenment through the most direct means (contemplation, meditation, intuition, etc.) **Mysticism:** Experiencing transcendental realities that lie beyond normal perceptual or intellectual apprehension (visions, divination, prophesy, etc.). Combining these elements does not connote that the terms are related, but simply that they have enough common esoteric qualities that a claim can be made that the terms are complementary. With both, you are asked to reach beyond the temporal and perceived realities of your consciousness to seek clarity and meaning to perplexing and enigmatic issues that pervade your thoughts and affect perceptions.

Ondas on Zen-Mysticism reflect the transcendental — that reality that is beyond what you have been led to believe, that defies your senses and that questions the nature of your existence. It is theoretical physics and quantum mechanics, with their own sets of enigmas, expressed in literary form. Some Ondas elicit meditation; others compel self-contemplation, while still others rub against the sensitive nerves of our intuition. In the case of these Ondas, it appears that they are what they are; discovering the "what" may be the biggest challenge.

CONCLUSION

The preceding mini exposition is my general attempt to describe something that is still as enigmatic as much as it is perplexing. Perhaps over time and further reflection the meaning and nature of Ondas will become more comprehensible. Because the future is to create and not to predict, the possibility is more probable than not.

MISSION

I profess belief in a divine energy greater than myself. My life-long love and interest in theoretical physics and quantum mechanics gives me a non-traditional understanding of the terms "divine" and "energy." To me, like a glittering diamond, the Divine has many gleaming facets, each with its own name. I see the terms "God" and "Great Spirit" interchangeably. Ondas with the term "God" are capitalize when referring to the supreme being of established religious faiths and use a lowercase "god" to refer to any supernatural, all-powerful entity or association with the idea of any similar concept of an omniscient entity.

To give you an understanding of my idea of the Divine, there is an Onda that reads,

ASPECT
You are a
Grain of sand
And God
Is the ocean.

Asking a grain of sand to explain the complexities of the seas is futile endeavor. Therefore, when I say what I am about to say, understand that the comments are coming from someone who sees himself as a grain of sand lying on a beach next to a vast sea that is an omniscient, divine and illimitable force. So, what does this have to do with the mission?

I was sitting on the floor and laid out in front of me were pages with literally thousands of Ondas that I had written over the first three or four years. Looking down at them, I was thinking about their nature when I had an epiphany and proclaimed to myself, "This is not your work!" quickly followed by, "Great Spirit I know this is your work. What am I supposed to do with these?" Before I had even finished asking the question, (my idea of) the Divine answered, "Share them with the world."

That is my mission, to share these and thousands of other Ondas with the world. And, among other things, to "share them with the world" dictates translating Ondas into other languages.

NOTE: (All good things cost and an ancillary mission is to make these Onda Collection books a financial success that will generate the resources necessary to find the freedom to devote myself full-time to this life-long endeavor.)

THE FUTURE

Plans are to create an online depository for the collection of Ondas along with an open invitation to the world to post their own Ondas (insights) on the same website. If any of the Ondas in this book or from an online feed pleases you, pass them on. If you begin experiencing and noticing your own Ondas, make note of them and share them with the rest of the world, too.

Help me share with the world the 366 Ondas you will find inside this book, as well as any other Ondas you may encounter.

Tito Pérez

ONDAS

2020 COLLECTION

REALISM

To the consciousness
reality is what it seems,
only life and death exist;
to the Spirit
reality is transcendental,
a piece of an infinite whole;
to the Soul
reality is itself,
everything else is illusion.

1

BENT

Humble trees
bend to the
will of the wind,
prideful trees
become firewood.

334

CONTINUE

Release

the past,

grasp

the present,

seek

the future.

338

ETHICAL

Ethics

limits the

amount of

available

options.

308

BITE

Forgive a snake
all you want,
but there
will be
a next time.

301

BLAMING

Often it is easier
to blame demonic
or evil forces
than to accept
culpability for one's
own and deliberate
improprieties.

302

FORGIVING

Forgive those who
know not
what they do,
pray to be forgiven
for things you did
when you too
did not know what
you were doing.

342

FAITHFUL

Start it

with faith,

say it

with words,

show it

with action.

309

HUMBLE

Humility

is a safe,

yet lonely,

place.

313

IMPORTANCE

Forgiving
is important;
not forgetting
sometimes even
more important.

314

INTELLIGENT

Intelligence is

relative to

time, place

and effort.

315

JOIN

Life is

a group

effort.

347

LOGICAL

Avoid using
logic and
everything
will appear
reasonable.

317

LOVES

Let they who
love
each other,
love
each other.

349

RISKY

You can
avoid all risks
by doing
absolutely
nothing.

325

GENTLY

First be

gentle with

yourself.

310

RESIDENT

God resides
outside your
imagination.

356

SLOWLY

There is

dignity in

slowness.

359

SOLVING

Violence has

never solved

anything that

reason could

not have

solved better.

360

SEEKING

Seek

happiness

more and

perfection

less.

326

SMALL

Consign yourself
to the reality that
you will always be
a smaller part of
something greater
than yourself.

329

TAKING

Only love
is taken more
for granted
than life.

330

SUMMATION

Reality is
the sum of your
rational thoughts
minus your
irrational emotions.

382

CONTRITE

Nothing disarms
quite as fast
as a sincere
act of contrition.

367

GREEN

Know that all

greener pastures

eventually turn

brown too.

371

CERTAINTY

The only thing
certain about
the future is
the uncertainty.

373

HATEFUL

Hate
is the most
hurtful of
all four-letter
words.

385

QUESTIONS

Ignorance
thrives best
where questioning
is absent.

384

INFECTION

Like the
worst of plagues,
Ignorance is
highly infectious.

394

SPOKEN

Speak the truth

as you

understand it,

not to

seek favor,

but to

be understood.

1500

TRIPPED

Because one
lie usually
follows closely
behind another,
they inevitably
trip each other.

418

UNDERSTOOD

Hope is an
understanding
with the self.

395

BLINDER

Love often
blinds one
to the truth.

415

TEMPTING

Temptation

always

approaches

with a

big smile.

361

STUDENT

The wisest of

the wise know

they really

know nothing.

1501

TRUTHFUL

The truth,
as you see it
is just that,
as you see it.

437

VOICES

Your

inner voice

does not waste

words or

your time.

439

CONSUMED

Anger

has a

ravenous

appetite,

it will

consume you.

458

MINDS

The mind

can be

convinced of

anything when

one has

no mind.

492

WAITING

It takes time

to believe

in one's self,

but time waits

for no one.

436

IMPOSSIBILITY

Believe in

the impossible

until all

possibilities

have been

explored.

453

LISTENS

The foolish

choose not

to listen.

465

SOURED

Bitter words
usually come
from angry
minds with
sour hearts.

616

LEADING

A leader is one
who has learned
to follow;
a follower is one
who is learning
to lead.

468

TEMPTED

Only the dead

no longer

succumb to

temptation.

498

IGNORANT

Intolerance:
The intractable
offspring of
ignorance.

1502

TIMELY

Give me time,
my God,
to sort
things out—
if not the time,
then give me
a quick end.

1503

APART

Love and distance
one can reconcile,
love and absence
only for a while.

494

SILENT

At times silence,
what is not said,
says more than
what is spoken.

474

SATISFIED

Hard work
combined with
satisfaction
always produces
the best results.

604

UNSOCIAL

Unfollow
a god that
judges,
unfriend
a god that
demands and
block
a god that
threatens.

620

BOX

A coffin
is a way
to hold
back nature
just a
little longer.

527

CRYING

No need
to cry
"Forgive us
Mother Nature!"
for nature
is unforgiving.

507

CREED

Do as
much good
while doing
as little harm
as possible
before dying.

1504

LIAR

You reach
a critical
juncture in life
when you begin
to believe your
own lies.

502

SUPER

There is no

supernatural,

everything is

natural even the

supernatural.

531

FEARS

The only
ghosts to fear
are those
from the
unrevealed
sins of
the past.

540

STRIVING

Prime-Directive:

Strive

to

survive.

181

APPRECIATING

Like a

dying ember,

learn to appreciate

the temporary

nature of

each precious

moment.

1505

DEPLETE

Earth will

give until

there is

no more

to give.

1506

DWELLING

Bad Karma
cannot dwell in
the house of
humility.

1507

TURNS

Be thankful
when your
world is
still turning.

987

CIRCLES

Death is
no more an
end then
birth is
a beginning—
parts of a
circle have
no start
or end.

1510

DREAMED

Everything

first originates

in a dream

or is

never born.

1508

MISUNDERSTOOD

How ironic

that our

very words

often prevent

us from

communicating.

1509

WASTED

Insults waste

breath,

time,

and

opportunity.

590

HUMANS

Great Spirit

I am mortal

let me

not forget,

I am human,

let me

always remember.

1511

DARE

You should
always continue
daring to believe
that one day
the world will
awake and find
that there is
no more
war or poverty.

1512

SAVING

Is it temperance
or temperament
that hold the key
to salvation,
or is it both?

591

TALKING

Some who

talk-the-talk

never even take

a step to

walk-the-walk.

598

INTER

To avoid

waking

the dead,

some bones

are best

left buried.

1513

OUCH

Be good
even when
it hurts.

624

BREATHLESS

Life is a
roller coaster
with many
ups, downs and
twist and turns
that take your
breath away.

596

VISTA

Lies with

panoramic vistas

receive the

most views.

619

POWER

Love is a
powerful hammer
that can knock
down any wall
if used
often enough.

608

ACCEPTING

Loving comes

easier to those

who do not

waste time

trying to

understand love

and just

accept it.

581

QUIETNESS

Some spend
time shouting
their faith;
others spend
time quietly
living it.

583

KILL

A truly
civilized society
is one that
does not tolerate
the killing of
its citizens by
anyone and
prohibits itself
from taking
life too.

638

BURNS

It would appear
some spend
entire lives
looking for
bridges to burn.

609

CRACKED

Physical love
eventually cracks
with wrinkles,
spiritual love
makes wrinkles
disappear.

633

DANCING

Even the

dead dance

to the

rhythm of

Karma's beat.

589

BOUND

The Soul and
eternity are
one and
the same.

665

ESCAPING

The most

liberating

freedom is

knowing that

you have

escaped your

own prison.

637

SPINNING

The young
believe the
world revolves
around them
until they come
to realize that
it is they who
revolve around
the world.

668

COMPUTING

The spirit is
an operating system;
the mind,
a hard-drive;
the conscious,
a processor;
and you
a computer.

648

DRIVE

Thoughts
driven by
emotions tend
to lose
control.

642

KARMIC

Poetic justice

is Karma in

real time.

643

CONSISTENT

None are more
consistently wrong
than those who
believe they are
consistently right.

646

SPEEDS

Depending on
attitude,
time can either
speed up or
slow down.

672

TASTE

Truth can be

sweet, bitter,

or bittersweet,

but never

tasteless.

674

GLORIFY

War is

to glory what

mayhem is

to peace.

675

TROUBLED

Trouble follows

those who

leave a trail.

679

SHATTER

Better to have
shattered dreams
than to have
no dreams at all.

654

VIOLENT

Violence is
the ultimate
act of control
by someone
out of control.

649

ADAPTING

When there
are many of
them and
few of you,
learn to adapt
or there may
be even
fewer of you.

677

RAGING

Rage is the

one emotion

that rapidly turns

calm reason into

frightful wrath.

653

POP

Inflated egos

are the

easiest

to burst.

682

STREAMS

Let your

stream of

consciousness

flow in

all directions.

658

UNDERSTAND

Great Spirit
let me not
die ignorant,
help me
recognize and
appreciate at
least one
simple truth
before my end.

1514

PASSING

After your death,
pray to be
remembered not
for who you were,
but for what
you became.

681

LUSTFUL

Most often
sex and lust
easily overcome
religious
convictions.

684

DWELL

Some spend
their lives
dwelling on a
promised heaven
instead of the
world that they
were given.

660

FLOW

Few possess
the tenacity
to swim against
the current,
most will be
swept downstream
with the
multitudes.

686

GUILTY

Time cannot

bury guilt,

only you

can put guilt

to rest.

662

AMORAL

A bad law
is one that
causes harm
when applied,
an immoral law
is one that
is applied
to cause harm.

663

ANSWER

Who says

you have

to respond

to every

question?

687

MOMS

Mothers will not
willing expose
a child to danger,
perhaps it is they
who should
decide the
necessity of wars.

664

ACKNOWLEDGE

Demonstrate your

intelligence by

acknowledging

your ignorance.

1515

DIVIDED

Religions have
served more
to divide and
less to unite.

693

APPRECIATION

Appreciate life—
acknowledge
the blessing,
accept
the challenge.

720

EXPRESSIONS

Though many

languages exist,

words express

similar thoughts,

sentiments and

feelings—

people all over

think, want and

feel the same.

722

MISSTEP

Until you can

assess the

difficulties of

someone's journey,

withhold judging

their missteps.

725

THUD

Compared to
the clanging
sounds of action,
words are just
dull thuds.

695

MAD

Anger can
be overcome
incrementally:
first pacify
your emotions,
second calm
your mind and
third temper
your actions.

723

HELPING

Beware of
preachers wearing
gold jewelry and
driving luxury cars
while asking you
for tithes for
their churches
and prayers for
the destitute.

727

FULL

If you cannot
fully comprehend
a problem,
you will never
fully recognize
a solution.

699

HOME

Question the motives of preachers who live in mansions while urging others to help the homeless.

701

RECOGNIZE

Blessed are
they who found
love and
recognized it;
not so
blessed are
they who had
love and
never knew it.

730

SHOUTS

Avoid clerics
who need
to shout
to be heard.

728

LOOPS

Careful your

learning curve

does not

turn into an

endless loop.

702

WALK

Do more
walking and
less talking and
you will get
to where you
want to go
much faster.

705

EXECUTE

State executions

in the name of

justice are

acts of vengeance

masked by law.

732

DETRACTION

Criticism of
others is
a good way
to detract
from your
own failings.

731

WORDY

Do not

attempt to

corner someone

with words

unless you

have a better

vocabulary.

733

TEARY

God does

not shed

happy or bitter

tears,

God does

not cry.

712

ENVIOUS

Envy is
not all bad,
who has not
envied the
power of
birds to fly?

737

HAPPENED

Everything does
happen for a
reason but
only when
it happens.

738

NOURISHING

Feed the

hungry and

nourish the

soul.

739

ILLUMINE

Great Spirit
I am lost
guide me
out of darkness,
shed light
on me that
I may find
my own way.

742

MATH

Everyone is
a mathematical
formula with some
formulas being
more complex
than others.

745

PREYING

In life there

are those

who prey

to survive

and those

who pray

they survive.

719

LOT

The Earth
is a tiny plot
situated in a
big neighborhood
called a solar system
located in a huge
community named
The Milky Way.

708

STUPIDITY

If you cannot
fix stupid,
you can
dismiss and
ignore it.

709

IMMOBILE

Even if you
do not know
whether you are
going in the
right direction,
know that
standing still
will not get
you anywhere.

746

PROTECTIVE

All religions
possess some
protectionist
tendencies,
some more
than others.

733

REASONED

Though everything
happens for
a reason
does not mean
you will ever
know the reason.

749

MOMENTS

We are
who and what
we are
from moment
to moment.

750

RELEASE

Sometimes

all you have

to do is

let go.

751

CYCLE

All things,
even the universe,
undergo some
form of
cyclic experience—
what goes around
eventually does
come around.

747

DEATH

When you
die in
your sleep
do you
wake up
dead?

775

PESTS

Perhaps it is
time to begin
asking how
long before
Mother Nature
tires of us,
deciding we
no longer
are welcomed.

776

SHOCK

No matter

how shocked,

God never

says "OMG!".

752

GLIMPSE

You are

blessed if in

your lifetime

you manage to

discern even a

glimmer of

absolute truth.

753

EXTREMES

Religions have
helped as many
people as they
have harmed,
religions are
inherently bipolar.

785

CONFLICT

If leaders
were compelled
to fight their
own wars,
conflicts would
be resolved
more quickly.

754

COLORED

Only the
colorblind truly
see all people
the same.

756

TRAVELS

If you travel
down the old,
worn paths of
the ancients,
how will you
ever discover
new trails?

757

RELIANCE

Since God has
done little to
end wars, famine
and poverty,
it appears God
is relying on
humanity to solve
its own ills.

760

SIMPLY

You can become
oblivious to the
beauty of
simplicity when
living in a
complex world.

761

WING

It is perilous
to ride on
the wings of
the dreams of
others.

767

RETURN

If you can
leave the world
with your soul
intact you will
not have to
come back
to recover the
missing pieces.

758

ALGORITHM

God uses

mathematics

to create

the seen and

the unseen.

786

SPECK

There are

more suns

than there are

grains of sand

and Earth is

a mote of

dust floating

in space.

794

INTENTIONAL

Love is

a deliberate

choice and

not a chance

occurrence.

770

AGED

Unlike
our bodies,
love can
grow stronger
with age.

771

LUCKY

Luck is

when you

challenge God

and are

given a pass.

772

HEARING

Many will
not listen
to themselves,
afraid to hear
what they
are saying.

822

WEAK

Many hide
weaknesses for
fear of discovery
that they are
human after all.

791

LOVED

Love is

an enigma

that may

never be

resolved.

795

SERVE

The three

pillars of

Public Service:

Industry,

Fidelity,

Integrity.

940

ROBED

Cleric robes

do not a

holy person

make.

799

KILLING

A major

difference:

animals

kill to live,

humans

live to kill.

802

GRACED

A prime
law of nature
dictates that you
begin to die
the moment you
are born,
the grace period
in between
is called life.

803

COSMOS

Matter and

antimatter

share opposite

sides of

the same

cosmic coin.

825

CULTURES

One culture

meeting another

culture creates

an opportunity

to form a

third culture

called unity.

826

ALLOW

A cardinal rule
declares we
should live
and let live,
from this creed
springs acceptance,
understanding
and peace.

828

COMMON

Remember

that in the

eyes of God

a "Holy Man"

is just

a man.

831

PRINCIPLES

1 - Live and let live;

2 - No harm, no foul;

3 - Keep the peace;

4 - Practice compassion;

5 - Exercise restraint;

6 - Follow the rules.

832

CRUISE

Many are
like passengers
on large ships
letting others
chart courses
for them.

813

TITLED

"Holiness",
"Excellency",
"Eminence":
Egotistic titles
humans bestow
on each other.

830

JUDGE

Judgmental
people
are unhappy
people.

809

THINK

Please

remember

not to

forget.

808

GUARDS

Soldiers that
stand guard
over peace
hold the most
critical watch.

812

ACCUSE

Those who
go looking for
fault in others,
always find
what they seek.

842

MASTERY

The true

master is

always a

student.

844

GLOOM

The only

darkness to fear

is the pall of

ignorance.

845

OPPRESS

The oppressed
often resist,
the suppressed
often insist,
the depressed
often desist.

624

CRUEL

There are

humans so

cold-blooded

that frost covers

their hearts.

1516

LIED

The lies

that haunt

the most are

the ones

that were

unnecessary.

1517

CHANGED

The degree
by which you
change is
equal to the
difference between
the force of
your desire and
the energy of
your resistance.

840

FACE

Confront and provoke
the dragon,
maybe it will
fly away;
if not,
stand and win, or
be prepared
to die.

41

HABIT

Recurring acts of honesty often lead to habits that become difficult to break.

879

FACADE

Arrogance and

vanity are

facades for

insecurities.

886

FEALTY

Be faithful

to your mate,

not to soothe

their soul, but

to save

your own.

888

DOMINANCE

The only time
religions are
a problem
is when
they dominate.

1524

PROPERTY

Females forced
to marry men
are chattel
first and
wives second.

851

EXCUSED

Any cause

that can justify

violence can

excuse other

mayhem too.

861

BLINDING

Blinded by
their religion,
many no longer
see the light.

892

CRITICAL

Because it is
easier to tear
down than
to build up,
many criticize
rather than
encourage.

304

ILLUME

The darkness of ignorance begins fading before the rising light of knowledge.

1518

TART

Deceiving
the self is
like biting into
a lemon and
calling it sweet.

929

BUGS

To survive
they adapt,
share and
cooperate—
ways in which
insects are
more advanced
than humans.

862

RETAIN

Attain,

maintain,

sustain.

863

CHARITABLE

Compassion is
the heart of
charity and
charity is the
manifestation of
compassion.

1525

PUSHED

Some often

find out

that apparent

pushovers are

not so easy

to push over.

902

SCOWL

Do not

cross

someone

wearing

a frown.

903

DEAD-ENDS

Every dead-end
has a starting
point to which
you can return.

906

THINKERS

The Great Spirit
communicates
more effectively
with those who use
their intelligence.

1519

LOUDLY

They who
shout to
declare their
faith do it
to hear
themselves.

1522

DIRGE

Death is

a musician

that plays only

one tune.

928

HURT

It is hurtful

to discount

the pain of

others.

1523

DISTURB

Agitation causes
ripples and
anger causes
waves on
the inner sea of
tranquility.

1520

ROOTED

If planted
deep within
the heart,
faith will
take root
and become
embedded in
the spirit.

936

HIDDEN

Genius
hides from
ridicule.

1521

SCRIBES

God bless the
free press—
bad grammar,
misspellings
and all.

———

918

DIAMONDS

Each soul is

a reflective

diamond facet,

some shining

more than

others.

932

CALLING

Except for
human beings,
every creature
is born knowing
its purpose
for living.

933

FACTS

Acquiring science-based knowledge is challenging, arduous work and reasons why religious fundamentalists avoid it.

934

FESTER

Guilt is like

an open wound,

the more

you ignore it

the worse

it becomes.

949

INTIMIDATE

How many
have come
close to glory
only to be
intimidated and
then turned
away?

955

VAINGLORY

They who look
themselves in
the mirror
to admire
themselves are
always pleased.

966

HUMBLEST

It is the least
humble who
proclaim their
humility.

938

MEDICATE

Laughter
is another
form of
pain medicine.

1526

SENSES

They without
a sense of
humor lack the
most important
sense of all.

1527

FAMED

Many seek the
comfort of
obscurity and
avoid the
glare of fame.

956

MOLDS

If God had
intended for
humans to be
one size, shape
or color, the
same would be
true with birds,
fish and insects.

984

PRAYING

In the end who
will be blessed,
those that lived
their days in
prayer or those
whose prayer
was in living?

1604

BROOD

Insects breed
in large
numbers as do
some humans.

974

LITMUS

When confronted

with challenges,

success is not

always determined

by victory, but

by the intensity of

your efforts

to overcome.

959

DEPENDENT

Freedom and

choice are

symbiotic words

that depend

on each other

to survive.

961

ADMITTED

If you look
back at life
and find that
you did wrong,
do not say you
were just human,
admit you
were just wrong.

871

NATURAL

It is an

abomination

to some that

same-sex humans

love each other,

nature dictates

attraction and not

the intolerant

divine rules of

bigoted humans.

991

VIEWS

Depending on
point of view,
god is either
a male, female
or both.

993

TRIPPING

It is your

failure to

learn from

your missteps

that can trip

you up again.

994

DIRECT

God guide
me in what
is good
and best,
I will do
the rest.

973

SEEING

It is easy
to see things
as they are;
often difficult
to see things as
they could be and
virtually impossible
to see things as
they will be.

976

HATING

Hatred is an

unnatural act,

a conscious

decision you can

choose not

to make.

1530

EMOTIVE

*An emotional
god is
more human
than god.*

996

CAUSE

It is better
to live for
than it is
to die for
good causes.

998

OFFENSE

Aggression
and retaliation
form a cycle
that has an
uncertain end.

1528

TREASURE

Knowledge,
wisdom and
understanding
are greater
treasures than
diamonds,
gold or money.

1529

BACKWARD

Sometimes
it is best
to take a
step back than
to turn the
other cheek.

978

RIDER

Life may be a

merry-go-round,

but nothing says

you have to

climb on.

1535

PI

Mathematics is
the language of
God and forms
the basis for
all divine
communication.

1537

EVIL

If all
human life
is sacred,
then any
form of
killing humans
is unholy.

1531

SCREAMS

Shouting or

screaming are

two ways to

make people not

want to listen.

1533

EQUAL

Only when
all wars have
ended and
everyone treats
each other
as equals can
humanity begin
to call itself
civilized.

1534

INTRINSIC

The only

thing God

sees as an

abomination

is ingrained

ignorance.

1539

LUST

Lusting is

crossing the

threshold from

spiritual to

physical love.

1541

SIMPLE

The fundamentalist
and the simpleton
share similar
views of the
world and of
creation.

1543

SNAPS

Those who
do not practice
critical thinking
resort to making
snap judgments
instead.

1536

REALITY

God protect
me from
realities that
are not of
my choosing.

1538

DESCEND

Blind faith

will always

lead you into

an abyss.

1540

TIMING

Yesterday is a

memory,

tomorrow a

possibility and

today a

certainty.

1545

DELAYED

Denial is

one way

to delay the

inevitable.

1546

SHAPED

Our bodies

are animated

pieces of clay

that others

try to shape

and form.

1547

PRIDEFUL

Pride is

an unstable

element,

too little or

too much

leads to

instability.

1544

JUST

The wheels of
justice turn slow
most times and
the wrong way
sometimes.

1548

BROKEN

Trust is
like a rock,
once shattered
it can never
be made
whole again.

1549

WISELY

The words of
the wise
comingle
with silence.

1550

POISE

When cast
with faith,
patience is
a spell that
will exorcise
the demons of
anxiety.

1551

PARROT

Parrots and
unthinking people
have much
in common,
both mindlessly
repeat words,
phrases and
gibberish.

1542

INVADE

To wildlife,

humans are

an invasive

species.

1556

EXPERIENCES

Time is an

impartial,

objective and

excellent

judge of

character.

1552

BEASTS

It should
be of little
surprise when
prisoners who
are treated like
animals live
by the law of
the jungle.

1554

NOVEL

Love stories take

on different

dimensions

when you

are one of

the main

characters.

1555

HI

Say hello

to love

every day,

while you

still can.

1557

BOIL

Cold, hard

truths can

make some

people

boiling hot.

1558

SILENCE

While the wise
remain silent,
fools proclaim
their wisdom
to the world.

1559

CALCULUS

Like clay,

God uses

mathematics

to shape

creation.

1560

PREDATOR

Predatory religions do not tolerate dissension, objection or the truth.

1565

HERETIC

Heretics and
infidels choose
to question
and not believe
while believers
accept and choose
not to question.

1556

ENMITY

Remove the
blinders of biases,
prejudices and
animus and you
will begin seeing
other humans
as equals.

1567

DRAMATIC

If you

take things

too seriously,

life can be

a series of

dramas.

1561

CHANGE

Neither swords,
guns or bombs
combined have
changed humanity
as much as
words.

1562

DECEIT

Deceitful people
become so
skilled they
often deceive
themselves.

1563

FACTUAL

Like oil
and water,
religious
beliefs and
science do
not mesh.

1568

POWERS

Trying to know
God is as easy
as a flea trying
to solve $E=MC^2$,
or a gnat trying
to fly to the moon,
or a sand crab
trying to explain
the complexities of
the seas.

1570

REVEL

Lest you

draw attention

to yourself,

it is unwise

to gloat when

bad Karma is

visiting your

enemies.

1571

PACE

Thoreau said
allow each to
march to the
beat of a
different drummer,
while in reality
many are forced to
keep step to the
cadence of others.

1564

PERFECTION

Nothing is
perfect in
nature except
nature itself.

1576

LINK

A prayer is
a bridge to
somewhere.

1577

LIES

It is easier

to run from a

lie than it is

to hide from

the truth.

1572

LIBERATE

You cannot

escape who

you are

but you can

break free

from yourself.

1573

BLOOMERS

Children cannot
be told when
to grow up
any more than
flowers can be
told when
to bloom.

1574

REVEALED

It is when

you first think

you know it all

that, at last,

you begin to

exhibit your

ignorance.

1680

APOSTATE

Many have
found clarity
and comfort
after turning
their back
on religion
and turning
their face
toward God.

1578

STRIFE

Having killed
each other by
the millions,
humans are not
a cooperative
species.

1579

DIRT

You and

everyone else

will be dead

and turned

to dust before

the biblical

end-of-times

ever arrives.

1575

PROMISE

Tomorrow

is not

promised,

make love

today.

1587

GUIDED

Great Spirit
I am lost,
guide me;
I am mortal,
strengthen me;
I am ignorant,
enlighten me.

1588

FOLLOW

Religious fundamentalists believe what they are told to believe.

1580

SINNERS

Religions provide

reset buttons

to forgive the

transgressions of

followers who

keep repeating

their sins.

1582

MOUTHY

Putting words
into someone's
mouth is one
way to win
an argument.

1583

CLOD

How arid the
thought that
having climbed
out of a
soup of mud
humans have
evolved to
little more
than clods.

1589

SHREDS

God, I pray
for the power
to shred
my past and
with the
pieces form
my future.

1590

FREE

Liberty
can have
no master,
nor can
freedom
be enslaved.

1591

WILLFUL

Many humans
have claimed
to have known
the will of an
unknowable god.

1584

CHOICE

You did not
choose to be
born but you
can choose
to live.

1585

EXPOSE

Your face

and eyes

might hide

your intent,

your actions

will not.

1586

INSPIRED

Action without
inspiration
is short-lived,
inspiration without
action will not
live at all.

1599

RECKONING

Love can make
the wise feeble,
turn joy into despair,
devour the spirit and
leave the soul
naked and bare:
love is a
force to be
reckoned with.

1592

OBTUSE

The ignorant
gravitate toward
the ignorant
perpetuating a
cycle of
ignorance.

1593

BEAUTIFUL

Vanity blinds

you to

the beauty

around and

within you.

1594

EXERT

What faith
and effort
cannot make
happen will
not happen.

1600

ACTIONS

Practice a

code of silence

with a

code of action—

let your acts

speak for you.

1601

NOBLE

To be of

service to

others is the

noblest of

endeavors.

1602

TURD

All humans

are turds

waiting to

happen.

1603

ILK

Intelligent and
ignorant people
gravitate toward
their own kind.

1595

ALGEBRA

You are an
algebraic formula
with your sum
being equal to
a fraction of
the whole.

1596

INVOKE

What humans
cannot fathom
they will conjure.

1597

GRACES

Divine grace

is not

proportionate

to the

intensity of

your prayers.

1605

REFLECTED

Tranquility is
a placid pool
whose mirrored
surface reflects
a calm spirit.

1606

INTOXICATE

Power is a

potent intoxicant

that can

inebriate and

debilitate.

1607

FATE

You are
not destined
to die,
you were
born to die,
what lies in
between is
destiny.

1598

OPENING

The light of
wisdom opens
your mind,
the light of
spirit opens
your heart.

1616

ACT

Without dreams
nothing can be,
without actions
nothing will be.

1617

MORTAL

In the end,
the most startling
conclusion you
may discover
is that you never
had a beginning
and have
always existed.

1608

BIAS

Objective

assessments

and rational

conclusions

rarely emanate

from pulpits.

1609

LEARNING

That violence

is not

an answer

is often

a lesson

the young

learn

first-hand.

1610

ANGRILY

Of all

emotions,

anger holds

the highest

order for

disorder.

1618

SEEKER

Some prefer
to seek
knowledge,
others prefer
to let
ignorance
find them.

1619

HYPOCRITE

The judgmental
tend to be
the hypocritical.

1621

APPEAL

Pray that

your enemies

pray for

peace too.

1622

ACTOR

You were
born to act:
the stage is set,
come out
from behind
the curtains,
play your role.

1611

ONENESS

You are:

One,

all,

everything,

nothing,

ordinary,

unique,

you.

1612

BIG

Your angel's

biggest

challenge is

you.

1613

INFECTED

Hatred is
a festering
spiritual boil that
eventually infects
the spirit.

1623

CALM

Controlling the

tongue starts

with the mind

and ends

with the silence.

1624

DAREDEVIL

They play
their game of
do or die,
the young
never ask why,
would you ask
"Why?" if you
were immortal?

1625

BEREFT

After dreams,
hope and
promise are gone,
if death does
not follow
surely despair
will.

1614

ILLUSORY

Perhaps love,

like reality,

is an illusion,

maybe love

exists only

when we

choose to

create it.

1615

TERRORIST

Terror is terror:
people wearing
pointy white hoods
or who don
black ski masks
are not out
to make friends.

1627

JOINED

Physical,
Spiritual—
The two
sides of the
love coin.

1635

BARRIERS

Dogmas turn
into walls
that religions
build around
themselves.

1636

WORK

Life is

a series of

workouts.

1638

BIASES

To survive,
humanity may
have to undergo
major attitude
adjustments.

1639

PESSIMISTIC

It is easier
to be a pessimist
and confirm your
fears than to be
an optimist and
affirm your faith.

1628

DEAD

This much
can be
said of death—
It leaves lasting
impressions.

1629

CARRIER

The Soul is

a vessel,

a cup whose

depth is

unfathomable,

whose rim

extends beyond

the mind's eye.

1630

AFFAIR

Infidelity and
bad Karma
sleep in the
same bed.

1640

DEFINED

Love

has many

definitions,

none of

them right.

1641

AGELESS

Time does

not effect

God's words,

but it does

their meaning.

1643

COMPREHEND

What you

want to

hear may

not be what

you need

to hear.

1644

TRAILS

Everyone

follows a

path in life,

the search

for meaning

is optional.

1631

GRADUALLY

God, if I

am destined

to slip

into oblivion,

let it be

down a

gradual slope.

1632

MEEKED

Mother Nature
must smile
at the notion
that the meek
shall inherit
an Earth she
will never
bequeath.

1633

REVERBERATE

Some words
will resonate
down the
chambers of
your mind
until you die.

1645

REGULATE

Be

safe,

alert,

attentive,

engaged and

sure of

yourself.

1646

LIST

Make

lists,

over

and

over.

1647

FEATS

Action is

the only

sound that

God hears.

1648

FOLLOWS

Avoid

following

mobs,

gangs

or other

followers.

1654

LOVINGLY

Love others

the way

they were,

the way

they are and

the way

they will be.

1655

UNCONDITIONAL

There are

no challenges

or barriers

that persistent

love cannot

overcome.

1658

LIMITED

Prayers are
bridges that
often cannot
be crossed.

1637

OUTCOME

God listens

to those

who speak

with actions.

1649

AGAIN

Forgiving
the same
thing a
second time
is a futile
gesture.

1650

WORKS

You are

a work

in progress

and will be

until you die.

1651

BOOK

Books

are the

life blood of

the mind.

1659

REVOLT

Better to
start than
to join a
revolution.

1661

DREAD

It is wiser
to fear Karma
than it is
to fear a god.

1663

ASSAULT

Violence is

a tool for

the spiritually

ignorant.

1665

VAIN

Vanity
resides on
the other
side of
a mirror.

1652

ASPECT

You are a

grain of sand

and God is

the ocean.

1653

SINCERELY

Nothing can

impower more

than sincere

forgiveness.

1657

FEARLESS

Karma

fears no

god.

1662

INTERACT

For mutual

good,

communicate.

1669

RESET

Another

day,

another

chance,

another

start.

1673

RULES

Life is short:
Engage,
contribute,
enjoy and
repeat until
you can
no more.

1675

IT

The ego
never wants
to let go of
itself.

1664

ACTUALITY

To some
God is
a creator,
to others
a dictator,
to most
God just is.

1671

STONES

When you

try again,

failure turns

into a

steppingstone.

1678

LED

Many find
it easier to
follow others
than to lead
themselves.

1679

CHALLENGED

Challenges
help you grow:
it may be
better to have
a mountain
to climb than
a small creek
to cross.

1667

ARRIVAL

When you lie
to others
Karma will visit,
when you lie
to yourself
Karma has arrived.

21

BEGET

The future is

not to predict,

but to create.

33

CARE

Fear not death
for its cold embrace
is inevitable,
be concerned
more with life
for its warm embrace
is not as certain.

136

CATALYST

Faith turns
mountains into mounds,
rivers into brooks,
oceans into puddles,
desperation into determination,
doubt into understanding,
weakness into strength,
fear into resolve and
prayer into a force.

5

GENESIS

We are born again
with each new sunrise,
that is the way it is,
that is the way
it has always been.

16

LISTEN

Communications
is a bridge you
should be able
to cross from
either side.

15

BIOGRAPHY

Legal Name: Margarito Pérez: named after grandfather who also gave him "Tito" nickname.

Pen Name: Tito Pérez

Birthplace: Born and raised around the cotton fields of the South Texas Coastal Bend.Major Oddities: (1) Two Birthdays: 1947; August 4th (legal) and September 4th (biological). (2) Declared legally dead by physician at 9 months old as a result of bout with polio; while doctor was telling parents that their son was dead, without permission an intern decided to inject adrenaline into his heart that brought him back to life.

Major Life Traumas: More surgeries and broken bones than he can count.

Major Life Milestone: Decided to start writing for "himself" on September 4th, 1997, his 50th "bio" birthday, with initial focus on poetry.

Major Discovery in Life: As a writer, finding his inner voice; as a human, finding out he was human.

Major Joy in Life: Family, pets, writing, independence.

Major Disappointment in Life: Yet to be encountered

Vocation: Educator/Writer (50+ years as educator and as a writer involving grants, proposals, research, speeches; resumes, etc., as well as poetry including spoken word.

Avocation: Pursuit of the luxury of time to write with reckless abandon.

www.ingramcontent.com/pod-product-compliance
Lightning Source LLC
LaVergne TN
LVHW020522100826
845148LV00010B/1309
* 9 7 8 1 7 3 6 7 8 7 0 0 7 *